DOUBLE BASS SOLO TECHNIQUES

A book of orchestral excerpts edited by

Keith Hartley

MUSIC DEPARTMENT

OXFORD

UNIVERSITY PRESS

OXFORD
UNIVERSITY PRESS

Great Clarendon Street, Oxford OX2 6DP, England
198 Madison Avenue, New York, NY 10016, USA

Oxford University Press is a department of the University of Oxford.
It furthers the University's aim of excellence in research, scholarship,
and education by publishing worldwide in

Oxford New York
Auckland Bangkok Buenos Aires Cape Town Chennai
Dar es Salaam Delhi Hong Kong Istanbul Karachi Kolkata
Kuala Lumpur Madrid Melbourne Mexico City Mumbai Nairobi
São Paulo Shanghai Taipei Tokyo Toronto

Oxford is a registered trade mark of Oxford University Press
in the UK and in certain other countries

ISBN 978-0-19-335911-6

Music origination by Barnes Music Engraving Ltd., East Sussex
Printed in Great Britain on acid-free paper by
Halstan & Co. Ltd., Amersham, Bucks.

CONTENTS

USEFUL TERMS

Double Bass, Contrebasse (*Fr.*), Kontrabass (*Ger.*), Contrabbasso (*It.*), Contrabajo (*Sp.*)

Orchestral performance terms

solo	One player only
soli	A solo for more than one player—sometimes the entire section
1. pult	Only the first desk/stand should play
1. metà (*It.*)/die Hälfte (*Ger.*)	Only the first player on each desk/stand should play
gli altri	All other players (i.e. those not playing a solo or soli line) should play
divisi (div.) (*It.*)/geteilt (get.) (*Ger.*)	The section should divide, usually within each desk/stand: the outside player takes the upper line and the inside player takes the lower line
tutti (*It.*)/alle (*Ger.*)	Everyone should play (e.g. after a solo or soli passage)
unison (unis.)	Everyone should play the same line (e.g. after a divisi passage)
tacet	Leave out/do not play

Bowing terms

arco	With the bow
du talon	At the heel of the bow
a punta d'arco	At the point of the bow
martelé	'Hammered'. Short, strongly accented notes played in the upper half of the bow
martelé du talon	Martelé at the heel of the bow
ricochet	Several notes repeated within a single thrown bow-stroke
spiccato (*It.*)/sautillé (*Fr.*)/ Spring Bogen (*Ger.*)	A fast, bounced bow-stroke that allows the hair to spring off the string
battute	Hit or strike the string with the hair in the upper half of the bow, often using repeated up-bows
col legno (*It.*)/geschlagen (*Ger.*)	Hit or strike the string with the wood of the bow
gestrichen (*Ger.*)	Bow the string with the wood of the bow. Not advisable to use your best bow!
tremolo (trem.)	Rapid repetition of a note or notes—sometimes referred to as 'scrubbing'
sul ponticello (*It.*)/sur le chevalet (*Fr.*)/ am Steg (*Ger.*)	Bow on (i.e. near) the bridge to produce a nasal or metallic sound. Often played in the upper half of the bow
sul tasto (*It.*)/sur la touche (*Fr.*)	Bow over the fingerboard. This is usually coupled with a low dynamic
naturale (nat.)	Discontinue any of the above and return to normal bowing
piqué ('shoe-shine')	Reverse the normal down–up bowing pattern to start with an up-bow

Pizzicato terms

pizzicato (pizz.)	Pluck the string
Bartók pizz. ó	Allow the string to snap against the fingerboard
pizz. arraché	'Torn' or 'snatched'. An extreme form of pizzicato, used by Debussy in *Pelléas et Mélisande*

Other terms

Hauptstimme	Main voice
Nebenstimme	Secondary voice
ottava (8va)	Play an octave higher than written
ottava bassa (8vb)	Play an octave lower than written
loco	Return to normal pitch (i.e. after 8va or 8vb)
suoni reale (*It.*)/hauteur réelle (*Fr.*)	Play the harmonics an octave higher than written
barré (*Fr.*)/parallel fingering	Use one finger to hold down several strings. This is particularly useful for intervals of a 4th
con sordino (con sord.) (*It.*)/ mit Dämpfer (*Ger.*)	Play with the mute
senza sordino (senza sord.) (*It.*)/ Dämpfer ab (*Ger.*)	Take the mute off
sul (*It.*)/sur (*Fr.*)	Play on the named string, e.g. sul G, sur La etc.
①	A circled fingering indicates a change in position
	A bracketed section should be played in one position

SLURRED BOWING

All the pieces in this section rely on seamless legato slurring. Move the bow across the string as smoothly as possible and aim to distribute the weight evenly across the length of the bow.

Overture *from* Le nozze di Figaro, K492

W. A. Mozart
(1756–91)

from Symphony No. 8 in B minor, 'Unfinished' D759

Franz Schubert
(1797–1828)

from Aida (Act IV)

Giuseppe Verdi
(1813–1901)

from Symphony No. 41 in C major, 'Jupiter' K551

W. A. Mozart
(1756–91)

To ensure there is no interruption of sound when slurring across the string, press down both notes together.
This applies particularly to intervals of 4ths (parallel fingering).

Rejoice Greatly *from* Messiah

G. F. Handel
(1685–1759)

from Symphony No. 39 in E♭ major, K543

W. A. Mozart
(1756–91)

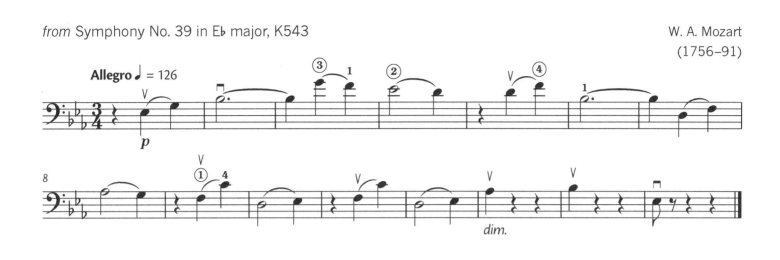

from Concerto pour la main gauche

Maurice Ravel
(1875–1937)

USING THE LOWER HALF OF THE BOW

Marcato: The following two examples introduce the basic orchestral off-string marcato stroke. Remain in the lower half of the bow, and use the weight of the stick to your advantage. In the Wagner, note the sequence of 4ths from bar 21. Remain in position for the bracketed notes.

from Die Meistersinger von Nürnberg (Act II)

Richard Wagner
(1813–83)

from España

Emmanuel Chabrier
(1841–94)

Repeated down-bows: In this next excerpt, keep the crotchets as long as possible by re-taking very quickly. Aim for the smallest of gaps between each down-bow, and take note of the accents.

from Symphony No. 2 in B minor

Alexander Borodin
(1833–87)

du talon/martelé du talon: Play the following examples on the string at the heel (du talon) of the bow. The martelé notes in the Brahms (bars 5–12) should be well marked and accented, to create a hammered effect.

from La mer

Claude Debussy
(1862–1918)

Variation VI *from* Variations on a Theme by J. Haydn

Johannes Brahms
(1833–97)

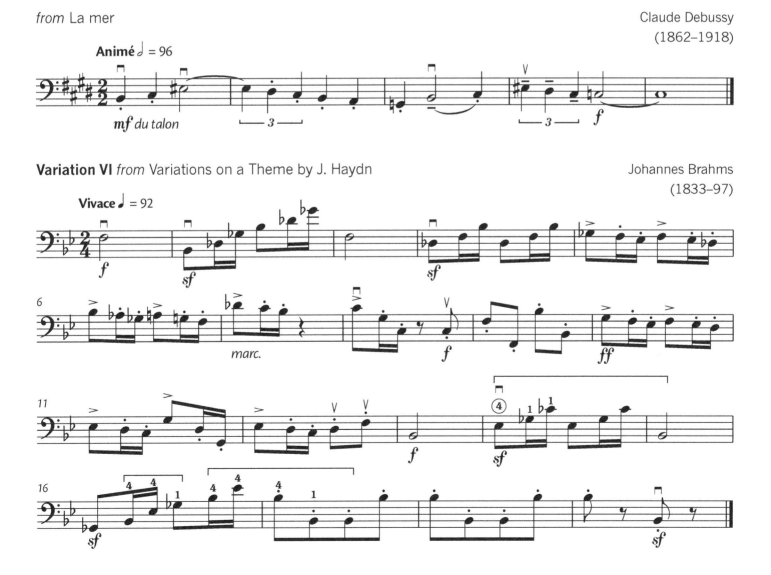

USING THE UPPER HALF OF THE BOW

Each of the following examples demonstrates the use of the upper half of the bow in a different way. In the Brahms, let the bow float lightly over the string, and note the use of short, accented up-bows in the Weber. The Bach requires a light, detached stroke.

from Symphony No. 2 in D major, Op. 73

Johannes Brahms
(1833–97)

Allegro con spirito ♩ = 104

Overture *from* Der Freischütz

C. M. von Weber
(1786–1826)

Molto vivace ♩ = 104

from Brandenburg Concerto No. 4 in G major, BWV 1049

J. S. Bach
(1685–1750)

Presto ♩ = 96

BOWING EFFECTS

Battute: Hit the string with the hair at the point of the bow (*a punta d'arco*), using repeated up-bows. The tautness of the hair will allow for a sharp, concentrated sound.

from Il Barbiere di Siviglia

Gioachino Rossini
(1792–1868)

Ricochet: Hit the string and allow the bow to bounce repeatedly within a single stroke. Experiment to find the ideal place on your bow (middle to upper half).

Overture *from* Guillaume Tell

Gioachino Rossini
(1792–1868)

Danse Espagnole *from* Swan Lake

P. I. Tchaikovsky
(1840–93)

Col legno: Hitting the string with the wood of the bow creates a percussive effect that is often called upon in orchestral writing. In these two examples, allow the bow to bounce repeatedly, in a similar way to ricochet.

Mars *from* The Planets

Gustav Holst
(1874–1934)

from Alborada del gracioso

Maurice Ravel
(1875–1937)

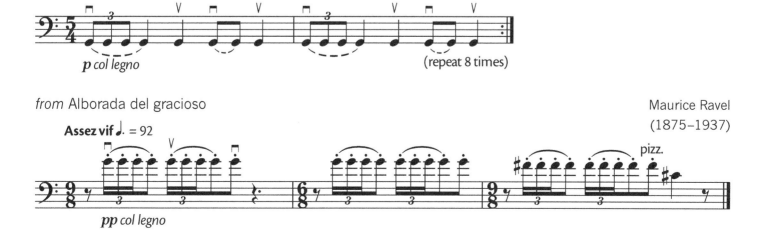

SPICCATO/SAUTILLÉ/SPRING BOGEN

Using the middle part of the bow, allow the hair to bounce off the string. (This technique is also used in 'Jeux d'enfants' in *Double Bass Solo 2*.)

from La traviata (Act II)

Giuseppe Verdi
(1813–1901)

from Octet in F major, D803

Franz Schubert
(1797–1828)

from Symphony No. 6 in B minor, 'Pathétique' Op. 74

P. I. Tchaikovsky
(1840–93)

The following two pieces continue the off-string spiccato bowing, but require more advanced string-crossing. Maintain control of the stroke by ensuring that the bounce stays in the centre of the bow.

from Falstaff (Act III)

Giuseppe Verdi
(1813–1901)

Scherzo *from* A Midsummer Night's Dream, Op. 61

Felix Mendelssohn
(1809–47)

BOWING DOTTED RHYTHMS

Hooked bowing: This bowing pattern presents one long and one short note 'hooked' or 'linked' together in a single bow-stroke. Take note of the wide variation in tempo markings in these examples and the different notation used by Brahms, Wagner, Mahler, Rimsky-Korsakov, and Schubert. (See also 'Euryanthe' in *Double Bass Solo 2*.)

from Symphony No. 4 in E minor, Op. 98

Johannes Brahms
(1833–97)

from Lohengrin (Act II)

Richard Wagner
(1813–83)

from Symphony No. 2 in C minor, 'Resurrection'

Gustav Mahler
(1860–1911)

from Sheherazade, Op. 35

N. A. Rimsky-Korsakov
(1844–1908)

from Symphony No. 9 in C major, 'Great' D944

Franz Schubert
(1797–1828)

Piqué ('shoe-shine') bowing: The traditional 'down–up' bowing pattern is reversed here. Play a short up-bow and a smoother down-bow. Look again at the last eight bars of the Schubert above, and try the alternative bowing marked beneath the notes.

from Symphonie fantastique

Hector Berlioz
(1803–69)

Slurred-in upbeats: The anacrusis/shorter note is now slurred onto the main beat. In the Musorgsky, watch out for the parallel 4ths and the quick changes between arco and pizz.

from Boris Godunov (Act III)

Modest Musorgsky
(1839–81)

from The Sleeping Beauty (Act III)

P. I. Tchaikovsky
(1840–93)

BOWING PATTERNS

This section introduces a variety of bowing patterns commonly called upon in the orchestral repertoire.
Practise slowly at first, and work up to the appropriate speed when the pattern feels comfortable. Watch out for
the *fp*s in the first excerpt—they occur on both down- and up-bows.

from Symphony No. 35 in D major, 'Haffner' K385

W. A. Mozart
(1756–91)

Overture *from* Don Giovanni, K527

W. A. Mozart
(1756–91)

Overture *from* Il Barbiere di Siviglia

Gioachino Rossini
(1792–1868)

* Extended or pivotal fingering: In this register, it should be possible for
most players to extend or pivot from D♯ to reach F♯ with the 4th finger
in bar 8.

from Symphony No. 40 in G minor, K550

W. A. Mozart
(1756–91)

from Symphony No. 88 in G major

Joseph Haydn
(1732–1809)

Overture *from* La forza del destino

Giuseppe Verdi
(1813–1901)

from Symphony No. 39 in E♭ major, K543

W. A. Mozart
(1756–91)

from Symphony No. 41 in C major, 'Jupiter' K551

W. A. Mozart
(1756–91)

from Serenade for Strings, Op. 22

Antonín Dvořák
(1841–1904)

from Piano Concerto No. 2 in B♭ major, Op. 19

L. van Beethoven
(1770–1827)

Fugue *from* The Young Person's Guide to the Orchestra, Op. 34

Benjamin Britten
(1913–76)

from Madama Butterfly (Act I)

Giacomo Puccini
(1858–1924)

Overture *from* Die Zauberflöte

W. A. Mozart
(1756–91)

'Amsterdam' rhythm: two hooked down-bows followed by an up-bow. After the long note keep the second down-bow as short and as tucked in as possible. (See also 'Die Walküre' from *Double Bass Solo 2*.)

from Octet in F major, D803

Franz Schubert
(1797–1828)

from Symphony No. 7 in A major, Op. 92

L. van Beethoven
(1770–1827)

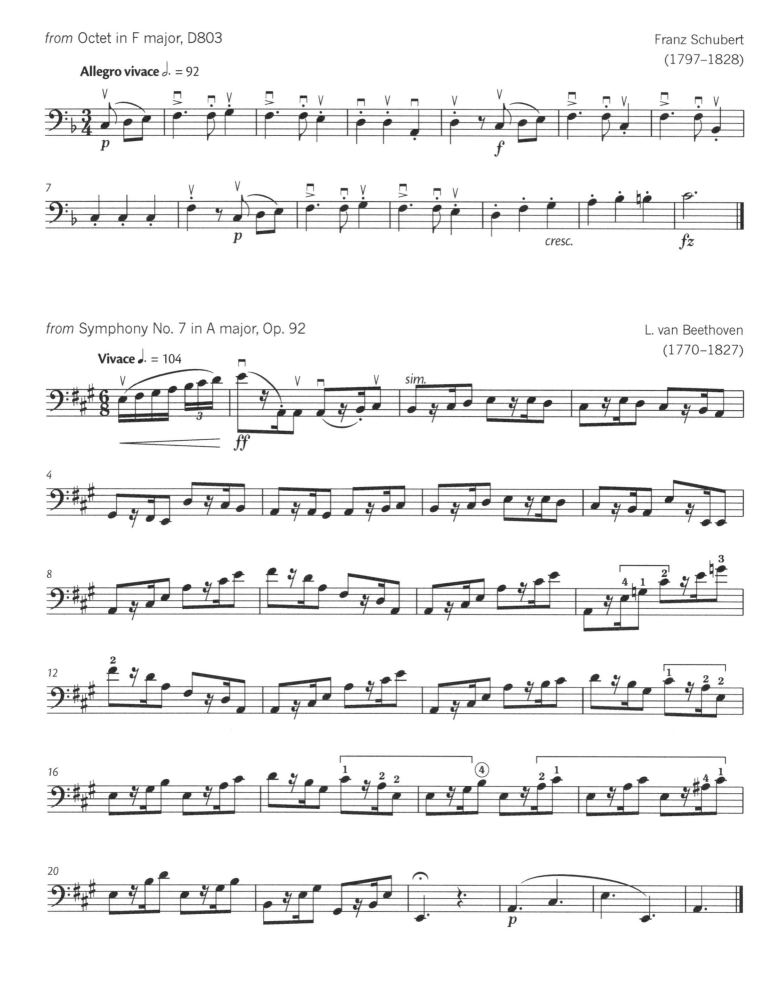

Now reverse the bowing so the stress falls on the 2nd beat of the bar. Start each group with a short, unaccented up-bow.

Vorspiel *from* Götterdämmerung

Richard Wagner
(1813–83)

from Symphony No. 4 in F minor, Op. 36

P. I. Tchaikovsky
(1840–93)

HARMONICS

Natural harmonics: These are produced by lightly touching the string at certain fixed points. They are referred to as 'natural' harmonics because they form part of the harmonic series of an open string, as opposed to a fingered or stopped note. Natural harmonics are often notated using a diamond-shaped note-head. Playing closer to the bridge will help to produce a clear harmonic sound.

The example below shows the natural harmonics available up to 4th position, including the standard tuning harmonics, which are indicated by a T. The lower line shows how the music would be notated (what you see on the page), and the upper line shows the pitches that would be created (what you hear).

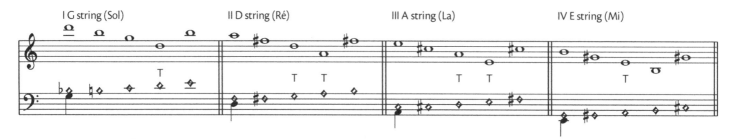

There are various ways to notate natural harmonics, and the examples below present alternative notations for a bar of *divisi* taken from Ravel's *La valse*. The first is Ravel's original, which uses the tonic sol-fa system to indicate the appropriate string for the harmonic.

Ravel made extensive use of harmonics, as in the following examples. Note that excerpt (b) from *Ma mère l'oye* can only be played on the C string extension.

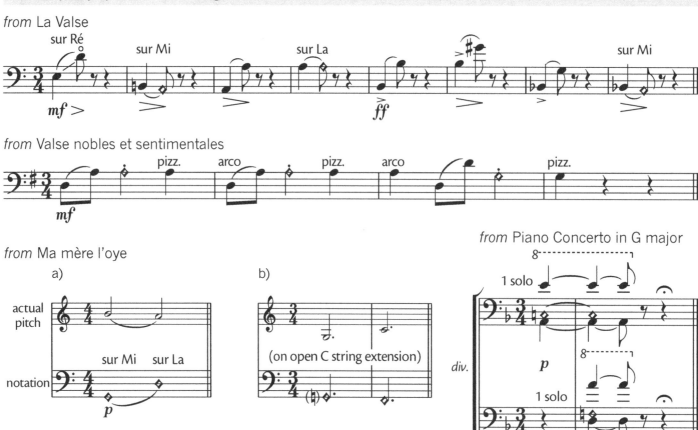

The following example presents the natural harmonics available in thumb position (an octave above the open strings). Three of the harmonics on each string occur at the same point as the equivalent stopped notes (these notes are starred).

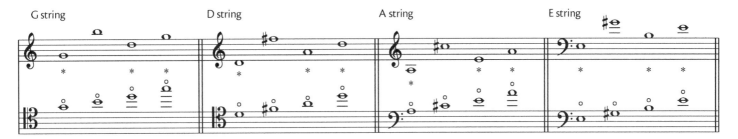

Artificial harmonics: Here the thumb presses down the lower note to create a normal stopped note, and the 2nd or 3rd finger lightly touches the string a 4th or 5th above. This type of harmonic is termed 'artificial' because the thumb essentially creates a new harmonic sequence by pressing down the lower note. This is a useful tuning position, producing notes one octave higher than the tuning notes on the previous page.

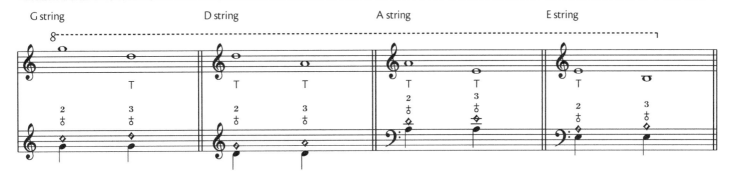

Ravel's *Le tombeau de Couperin* includes a famous passage of harmonics—both natural and artificial. This excerpt lies comfortably under the fingers in thumb position, despite what it looks like on the page! The upper line indicates the thumb-position fingering, while the lower line shows Ravel's notation.

Menuet *from* Le tombeau de Couperin

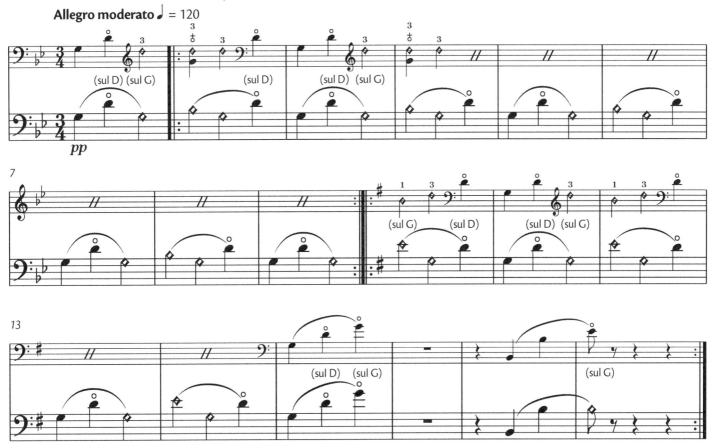

The following harmonics are found in the highest thumb position. Despite the difficulty of being higher up the fingerboard, the harmonics are much more willing to sound in the upper register.

from Concerto in A major

Domenico Dragonetti
(1763–1846)

Suoni reale/hauteur réelle: These terms indicate that a passage is to be played one octave higher than written.

Prelude *from* Agon

Igor Stravinsky
(1882–1971)

from L'enfant et les sortilèges

Maurice Ravel
(1875–1937)

Glissando (gliss.): This glissando is made up of a harmonic sequence. Glide the finger over the string, without pressing down, and the harmonics will ring out individually.

from L'heure espagnole

Maurice Ravel
(1875–1937)

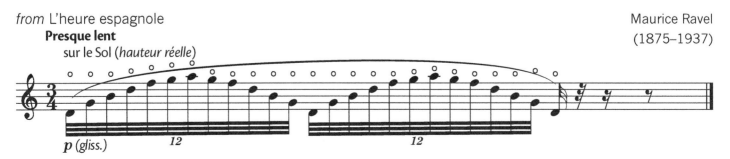

TENOR AND TREBLE CLEFS

The upper registers of the bass are usually notated in the tenor or treble clef. When playing high on the fingerboard, keep the bow near to the bridge to maintain clarity of sound. The symbols H⌐ and N⌐, meaning 'Hauptstimme' (main voice) and 'Nebenstimme' (secondary voice), were used by Alban Berg to indicate the relative importance of certain melodic lines.

from Drei Orchesterstücke, Op. 6 — Alban Berg (1885–1935)

from Wozzeck (Act III) — Alban Berg (1885–1935)

from Katya Kabanova (Act III) — Leoš Janáček (1854–1928)

Variation XI *from* Variaciones concertantes, Op. 23 — Alberto Ginastera (1916–83)

Ginastera: © Copyright 1954 Boosey & Hawkes, Inc. Copyright renewed.
Reproduced by permission of Boosey & Hawkes Music Publishers Ltd.

PIZZICATO TECHNIQUES

The bass-line from Bach's 'Air on the G String' was originally bowed, but the pizzicato version serves as an excellent exercise for working on a sustained pizzicato sound and the tuning of octaves. In the Janáček, use the 4th finger as a bar (barré) across the G, D, and A strings.

from Suite No. 3 in D major, BWV 1068

J. S. Bach
(1685–1750)

from Sinfonietta

Leoš Janáček
(1854–1928)

Pizzicato tremolo: This rhythmic pizzicato is sustained throughout the violin cadenza passages of *Sheherazade*. A similar style is also found in the accompaniment to the cadenza in Elgar's Violin Concerto.

from Sheherazade, Op. 35

N. A. Rimsky-Korsakov
(1844–1908)

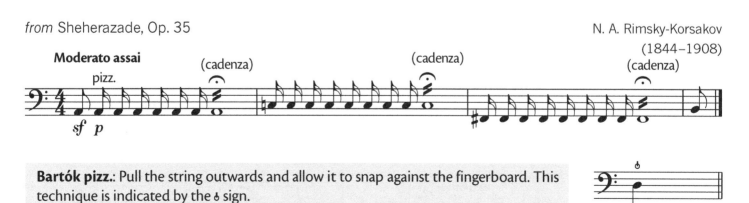

Bartók pizz.: Pull the string outwards and allow it to snap against the fingerboard. This technique is indicated by the ↕ sign.

Scherzo *from* Symphony No. 4 in F minor, Op. 36

P. I. Tchaikovsky
(1840–93)

Left-hand pizz.: To allow time to prepare the bow for the arco notes, use the left hand to pluck the open strings marked 'L.H.'.

from Daphnis et Chloé

Maurice Ravel
(1875–1937)

LEFT-HAND TECHNIQUES

Acciaccatura and appoggiatura: When a small note has a line through its tail (acciaccatura), it should be 'crushed' against the main note; when there is no line (appoggiatura), the small note takes half the value of the main note.

from The Nutcracker

P. I. Tchaikovsky
(1840–93)

from Violin Concerto No. 5 in A major, K219

W. A. Mozart
(1756–91)

Turn/gruppetto and trill/shake: The small notes in the examples below show the patterns to be used for each turn/trill. Note the use of accidentals with both the ∾ and *tr* symbols.

Romance *from* Eine Kleine Nachtmusik, K525

W. A. Mozart
(1756–91)

from Symphony No. 2 in D major, Op. 36

L. van Beethoven
(1770–1827)